Better Homes and Gardens®

TREES SHRUBS AND ROSES

Excerpted from Better Homes and Gardens® *STEP-BY-STEP SUCCESSFUL GARDENING*

BETTER HOMES AND GARDENS® BOOKS

Editor: Gerald M. Knox
Art Director: Ernest Shelton
Managing Editor: David A. Kirchner
Editorial Project Managers: James D. Blume, Marsha Jahns,
    Rosanne Weber Mattson, Mary Helen Schiltz

Garden, Projects, and New Products Editor:
    Douglas A. Jimerson
Associate Editor: Jane Austin McKeon

Associate Art Directors: Linda Ford Vermie,
    Neoma Thomas, Randall Yontz
Assistant Art Directors: Lynda Haupert, Harijs Priekulis,
    Tom Wegner
Graphic Designers: Mary Schlueter Bendgen, Mike Burns,
    Brian Wignall
Art Production: Director: John Berg;
    Associate: Joe Heuer
    Office Manager: Michaela Lester

President, Book Group: Fred Stines
Vice President, General Manager: Jeramy Lanigan
Vice President, Retail Marketing: Jamie L. Martin
Vice President, Administrative Services: Rick Rundall

BETTER HOMES AND GARDENS® MAGAZINE
President, Magazine Group: James A. Autry
Vice President, Editorial Director: Doris Eby
Executive Director, Editorial Services: Duane L. Gregg

TREES, SHRUBS, AND ROSES
Editorial Project Manager: Rosanne Weber Mattson
Graphic Designer: Brian Wignall
Electronic Text Processor: Paula Forest

CONTENTS

TREES IN THE LANDSCAPE

Before you select a new tree, consider these variables: the mature height, which needs to be in proportion to the surroundings; the shape, which can be columnar, globular, or horizontal; and its intended use, such as screening, shade, or flowers. Evergreen trees will work best for screens or windbreaks; deciduous trees offer the advantages of bright autumn foliage color.

If you're still uncertain about what type of tree to plant, let the size and style of your house decide for you. Towering shade trees blend well with big homes on large lots. The stately old oak *opposite* protects this house from the elements. In the summer, its leafy shade helps keep down the temperature indoors. In the winter, its bare branches let the warm sunshine through.

Small trees work well on pocket-size lots. Appearing each spring as a cloud of white, the fragrant blossoms of the cherry tree *below* make a delightful contrast against the deep red leaves of Japanese maple. Other good choices are dogwood, redbud, flowering crab, star magnolia, and amur maple.

TREES IN THE LANDSCAPE

Consider the seasonal qualities of trees before you make your final selections. You can create an attractive all-season landscape by choosing a variety of shade and ornamental trees with different appealing qualities.

SPRING BLOOM
■ You know it's spring when certain ornamental trees burst into bloom. Favorite spring-blooming trees are redbud, dogwood, pear, flowering crab, acacia, horse chestnut, hawthorn, and tulip tree. Fruit trees, including apple, peach, cherry, and plum, will add their own colorful charm.

SUMMER BLOOM
■ Long, hot days can be brightened with a selection of summer-flowering trees. Crape myrtle, golden-rain tree, golden-chain tree, stewartia, silk tree, Japanese tree lilac, and catalpa are popular species in this category.

FALL FOLIAGE AND BERRIES
■ Many trees have breathtaking autumn leaf color. If yellow and gold are your favorite fall hues, choose ash, beech, birch, butternut, ginkgo, hickory, honey locust, linden, sugar maple, pecan, poplar, tulip tree, and walnut. If you prefer red tones, pick dogwood; hawthorn; sophora; red maple; pin, red, and scarlet oak; sour gum; sourwood; and sweet gum. Bright orange foliage graces yellowwood, Ohio buckeye, and paperbark maple. The sourwood (sorrel tree) blooms in fall at the same time that its foliage turns red.

Fall also is a time for fruits and berries. These often hang on well into winter and provide color against a snowy landscape. To add fruits and berries to your landscape, select trees such as dogwood, hawthorn, Russian olive, holly, flowering crab, sourwood, golden-rain tree, and mountain ash.

WINTER INTEREST
■ The pageantry of trees doesn't have to close down for the season when winter arrives. You can add interest to an otherwise dreary landscape with colorful or patterned bark or an unusual trunk shape. Beautiful bark is found on crape myrtle, birch, beech, sweet gum, sycamore, willow, cherry, and eucalyptus. Trees with attractive silhouettes include weeping cherry or birch, crape myrtle, katsura tree, dogwood, magnolia, poplar, zelkova, and tulip tree. Evergreens add color to a snowy yard by keeping their foliage year-round.

ALL-SEASON INTEREST
■ Many trees will give you the best of all worlds by offering color and interest every season through flowers, foliage, fruit, and bark. The dogwoods *below* display white flowers in spring, scarlet leaves in fall, and wine-colored berries in winter to make a striking year-round accent. Other top choices are sweet gum, crape myrtle, sourwood, hawthorn, holly, and pear.

Trees that bear fruit or nuts are a natural source of food for wildlife. To attract winged and four-legged creatures to your yard, plant such trees as red and white oak, red maple, white pine, hemlock, birch, Russian olive, amur maple, blue and Norway spruce, beech, red cedar, serviceberry, mountain ash, hawthorn, dogwood, flowering crab, hackberry, and mulberry.

Small trees are ideal for small lots because they won't interfere with other gardening. The redbud at *left* works exceedingly well as an accent in a bulb border; redbud's canopy of leaves will appear after the blossoms of the sun-loving tulips and daffodils have faded.

Many people thrive on city life, but some tree species can't adjust to the soot and grime of the urban environment. Shade trees that have proved to be tolerant to air pollution include Norway maple, honey locust, little-leaved linden (it is sensitive to salt compounds—don't plant it along a street or walkway that might be salted during the winter), ginkgo, pin oak, Austrian pine, willow, horse chestnut, hackberry, and ash.

Choose a tall, columnar evergreen if you want to soften a wall or hide an eyesore. The pyramidal Chinese junipers planted in the narrow strip between driveways at *left* offer both privacy and a refreshing break from an otherwise humdrum landscape plan. A mulch of chipped bark keeps weeding and watering to a minimum.

Keep evergreens pruned to retain an appropriate shape and size for their location in your landscape. Once oddly shaped and overgrown, evergreens usually are hard to restore.

Other plants that can be used for effective privacy screening include poplar, hemlock, arborvitae, podocarpus, and cypress. Fir, cedar, pine, juniper, holly, false cypress, and eucalyptus are equally attractive when planted close together to act as a tall hedge.

GALLERY OF TREES

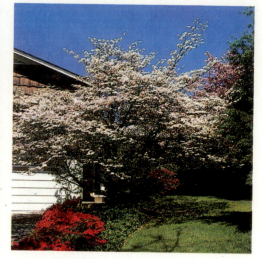

BIRCH
Betula species

Birches are a group of attractive, relatively short-lived trees used for their decorative qualities. The bark of the paper or canoe (*B. papyrifera*), weeping (*B. pendula*), and gray (*B. populifolia*) birches is white; the bark of the river birch (*B. nigra*) is chocolate brown.

SOIL: River birch: wet; canoe and other birches: prefer moist soil, but tolerate other soils

LIGHT: Full sun to light shade

HARDINESS: Zone 2 to 4

COMMENTS: The river and canoe birches are the largest growing, reaching up to 90 feet tall. Weeping birch is next in size, reaching up to 50 feet high. The gray birch is the smallest at about 25 feet tall. The canoe birch grows in clumps of two to four trunks; the weeping birch has the characteristic pendulous branches.

CRAB APPLE
Malus species and hybrids

Crab apples are showy, small trees with white, pink, or red single, semidouble, or double flowers in mid-spring. Decorative and edible red, yellow, or green fruit forms in early fall. Fruit is bitter but can be used in jams or jellies. Crab apples reach 15 to 25 feet in height and have a wide spread.

SOIL: Rich, well drained; tolerates acid, alkaline, or wet

LIGHT: Full sun

HARDINESS: Zone 3 to 5

COMMENTS: It's common to have crab apples bloom profusely one year and then not bloom well the next. Good choices include: the white Japanese crab apple (*M. floribunda*); the red Hopa; the pink tea (*M. hupehensis*); the white Sargent (*M. sargenti*); and the Red Jade with white flowers and bright red berries on weeping branches.

DOGWOOD
Cornus species

Dogwoods are showy, highly prized for landscaping, and valued for their size, shape, flowers, fall foliage, and bright berries. The two major tree species are the flowering dogwood (*C. florida*) and the Japanese dogwood (*C. kousa*). Flowers are white or pink, with four rounded petals in mid-spring. The Japanese dogwood blooms about a month later, with larger, pointed, white flowers. Both reach about 20 feet in height, and produce architecturally interesting, horizontal branches.

SOIL: Rich, well drained, slightly acidic, moist. Add magnesium for bloom.

LIGHT: Full sun to part shade

HARDINESS: Flowering, Zone 5 Japanese, Zone 6

COMMENTS: Buds form in fall with the berries and scarlet leaves. The best spring flowers follow hot, dry falls.

GINKGO
Ginkgo biloba

This tree—also known as the maiden-hair tree—is tough and attractive, especially in fall, with its golden foliage. The leaves are fan-shape, like those on the maidenhair fern. Trees can reach 75 feet high but usually do not grow taller than 50 feet. This slow grower is an excellent lawn or street tree because of its high tolerance of pollution. Young trees have an awkward shape. Plant only male trees, as the female has a fruit with an unpleasant odor.

SOIL: Deep, loose, well drained. Water heavily after planting.

LIGHT: Full sun to part shade

HARDINESS: Zone 5

COMMENTS: Ginkgo has always been rated as one of the best urban or city trees. It is relatively pest-free. In the fall, all the leaves drop at the same time, making raking easier.

GOLDEN-CHAIN TREE
Laburnum species

The golden-chain tree is best known for the long—12- to 18-inch—clusters of yellow, pealike flowers in mid-spring that resemble wisteria blossoms. After blooming, the tree has little interest and no fall color. The mature height of the golden-chain tree is about 30 feet. The leaves are bright green and cloverlike on branches that generally grow upright but sometimes develop into a shrubby form. There are two available types: the common golden-chain (*L. anagyroides*) and a hybrid (*L. x watereri*), which many gardeners claim as the better of the two.

SOIL: Well drained, moist, acidic

LIGHT: Full sun to light shade. Do not use in hot afternoon sun.

HARDINESS: Zone 6

COMMENTS: Frequent pruning might be needed to keep plants in shape. The seedpods, which form in the fall and cling until midwinter, are poisonous.

HAWTHORN
Crataegus species

Hawthorns are small and decorative trees, reaching about 25 feet in height and spreading up to 20 feet wide. They are known for their late-spring white or pink flowers and bright red or scarlet berries—the berries may remain on the limbs all winter. All hawthorns except the English turn bronze or orange in fall. The plants have stiff thorns along the branches.

SOIL: Prefer poor, dry soils.

LIGHT: Full sun or light shade

HARDINESS: Zone 5

COMMENTS: Many excellent hawthorns are available. Their major problem is a susceptibility to fire blight. Choose between the cockspur (*C. crus-galli*), Lavalle (*C. x lavallei*), English (*C. oxyacantha*), or Washington (*C. phaenopyrum*). Good hybrids include Autumn Glory, Toba, Winter King, or Paulii (Paul's Scarlet), a variety that does not form fruits.

GALLERY OF TREES

MAGNOLIA
Magnolia x soulangiana

The common or saucer magnolia is named for the saucer-shaped, pale pink flowers that appear in early spring. These blooms can be up to 6 inches across and appear before the 6- to 8-inch leaves. A late frost, snow, or heavy wind may ruin the flower show. Magnolias grow to about 30 feet.

SOIL: Rich, well drained, moist
LIGHT: Full sun or light shade
HARDINESS: Zone 6
COMMENTS: Plant magnolias where they will be protected from late frosts. The saucer magnolia has several relatives worthy of a spot in the landscape. The star magnolia (*M. stellata*) blooms a little later than the saucer, showing off white flowers with straplike petals. The Southern magnolia (*M. grandiflora*) has huge, glossy evergreen leaves, along with enormous fragrant, white flowers in late spring and summer. However, the Southern magnolia is hardy only to Zone 7.

MAPLE
Acer species

Maples are a large species of trees generally used for shade or planted along a street. They vary in size and are best known for their attractive, deeply lobed leaves that present outstanding fall color. Species like the Norway maple make excellent street trees.

SOIL: Tolerant of many soils, but most prefer moist soils.
LIGHT: Full sun or light shade
HARDINESS: Zone 3 to 6
COMMENTS: The most popular maples are: Norway (*A. platanoides*), one of the best with many fine hybrids; sycamore (*A. pseudoplatanus*); red or swamp (*A. rubrum*), especially good in wet areas; silver (*A. saccharinum*), weak-wooded and weedy; sugar (*A. saccharum*), another of the best maples and the source of maple syrup; Japanese (*A. palmatum*), a smaller, often red-leaved decorative tree; paperbark (*A. griseum*), with shedding bark; amur (*A. ginnala*), the most hardy; and black (*A. nigrum*).

MIMOSA (silk tree)
Albizia julibrissin

This quick-growing lawn or specimen tree grows about 20 to 25 feet high, with the top forming an umbrella almost as wide. The leaves are large—up to 12 inches long—and fernlike. In the summer, pink flowers, resembling pincushions or powder puffs, appear. This tree creates light shade but is best used ornamentally. The flowers tend to drop and be somewhat messy in summer, so don't plant it too close to patios, driveways, or outdoor living areas. Multiple stems may form but should not be allowed to branch close to ground. After blooms fade, long seedpods form.

SOIL: Prefers poor, dry soil.
LIGHT: Full sun
HARDINESS: Zone 7
COMMENTS: The mimosa does best where summers are hot. The light-sensitive leaves fold up at night.

MYRTLE, CRAPE
Lagerstroemia indica

This small tree or shrub is best loved for the clusters of flowers that appear in late summer. Blooms can be red, rose, pink, lavender, purple, or white. The individual blooms look like crepe paper and the cone-shape clusters can be up to 12 inches long. As a tree, crape myrtle reaches 25 feet tall and develops vase-shape branching. The trunk and branches are covered with an attractive, shedding bark. Very often the tree is multitrunked. Fall color is not one of this tree's assets.
SOIL: Dry, acidic
LIGHT: Full sun
HARDINESS: Zone 7
COMMENTS: Since the crape myrtle blooms in the summer on new wood, it should be pruned in early spring to keep it compact and to correct its shape. It prefers a hot, dry climate and may be subject to mildew in damp areas. In areas of marginal hardiness, it may die to the ground in winter.

OAK
Quercus species

Oaks are deciduous or evergreen trees valued both for their wood and their shade and decorative assets. All popular types grow tall, up to 60 feet. Foliage is lobed, and most types have good fall color. Oaks are long lived, deep rooted, and an excellent landscape tree.
SOIL: Acidic, moist, well drained
LIGHT: Full sun or light shade
HARDINESS: Varies
COMMENTS: Choose from the following: White (*Q. alba*) is slow growing but majestic when mature—Zone 5; scarlet (*Q. coccinea*), fast growing—Zone 4; bur (*Q. macrocarpa*), one of the largest and hardiest; pin (*Q. palustris*), one of the best shaped trees for street plantings—Zone 5; English (*Q. robur*), one of the most highly hybridized—Zone 5; red (*Q. rubra*), one of the fastest growing—Zone 5; live (*Q. virginiana*), one of the few evergreen oaks—Zone 7; willow (*Q. phellos*), a slender grower with narrow leaves—Zone 6.

PINE
Pinus species

Pines are needle evergreens. Although the group contains a few shrubs, most are trees. Pines are classified by their cones and by the number of needles per bundle on the branches. They vary in height, hardiness, and shape. All can be pruned by cutting back the candles that form each spring.
SOIL: Well drained, low in fertility
LIGHT: Full sun
HARDINESS: Varies
COMMENTS: Choose one of the following species for your landscape: Scotch (*P. sylvestris*) grows to 80 feet, with drooping branches—Zone 3; Eastern white (*P. strobus*) grows to 100 feet, with fine-textured needles—Zone 4; Austrian (*P. nigra*) grows to 90 feet, with stiff needles—Zone 5; Swiss mountain or mugo (*P. mugo*), a compact grower to 25 feet—Zone 3; Himalayan (*P. griffithi*), one of the largest, growing to 150 feet with very long, drooping needles.

11

GALLERY OF TREES

PRUNUS species
Cherry, plum, peach

Within this genus of fruit trees are a number of ornamentals grown for their spring flowers. These are low-growing, decorative trees, reaching about 20 to 25 feet in height and blooming in mid-spring. These trees do not bear fruit.

SOIL: Fast draining
LIGHT: Full sun
HARDINESS: Zone 6
COMMENTS: There are several species of flowering cherries. The upright, stiff tree with the large, double, pink blooms is the Oriental or Kwanzan cherry (*P. serrulata*). As the tree matures, its shape becomes rounder. The finer textured pendulous cherry is the Higan (*P. subhirtella*). Its flowers are a very pale pink. The flowering peach (varieties of *P. persica*) blooms a little earlier and has deeper pink to red flowers. The flowering plum (*P. cerasifera*) has pink flowers and purple foliage.

REDBUD
Cercis canadensis

The eastern redbud is one of the first trees to bloom in the spring, with small, purplish pink, pealike flowers that bloom along the branches before the leaves appear. Redbud grows 25 to 30 feet tall and has stiff branches that create a horizontal configuration. Seedpods form in fall along with bright yellow autumn color on heart-shape leaves. Varieties with white or pure pink flowers also are available.

SOIL: Tolerant of any soil.
LIGHT: Sun or shade
HARDINESS: Zone 5
COMMENTS: This early bloomer has interesting branching even in winter. Varieties available include Alba, with white flowers; Flame, with the same color blooms but straighter growing; Pink Charm, with pale pink flowers; and Oklahoma, with red blooms.

SPRUCE
Picea species

The spruces are not always the best trees for a small landscape. They are stiff, upright trees with sharp needles and cones that hang down (by comparison, fir tree cones stand upright). Spruce trees often are quite large and out of proportion to other plants in the landscape. Most types reach a height of 100 feet or more.

SOIL: Prefer cool, moist soil.
LIGHT: Full sun
HARDINESS: Zone 3
COMMENTS: The best spruces for the garden are: Colorado blue spruce (*P. pungens glauca*), with stiff needles and blue-gray color; Alberta (*P. glauca conica*), a compact grower with bright green tufts of needles; Norway (*P. abies*), fast growing, wind resistant, with attractive, drooping branches; Serbian (*P. omorika*), a narrow grower and one of the best for the garden.

SUMAC
Rhus copallina

Sumacs are large, fast-growing trees and shrubs that can quickly outgrow their place in the home garden. They are best known for their large, compound, shiny, dark green summer leaves and brilliant, deep red fall color. These trees can grow to 30 feet, but can be kept as a low-growing tree about 10 to 15 feet tall. They may have a few flowers and red berries in summer.

SOIL: Poor, dry soil

LIGHT: Full sun. Will grow in shade but will lose their color.

HARDINESS: Zone 5

COMMENTS: This plant will do especially well along slopes and in wooded situations. If soil is too good, the plant will not do well. This plant is related to poison ivy, poison oak, and poison sumac, but is not poisonous itself. Give it room to grow for best results.

TULIP TREE
Liriodendron tulipifera

This fast-growing tree reaches 75 feet in height. You'll appreciate its beauty more if you don't crowd it. The main attraction of this tree is its pyramidal, symmetrical shape clothed in bright green, large, fan-shape leaves. Another asset is the large, pale yellow, tulip-shape flowers that bloom in mid- to late spring. Foliage turns yellow in fall to complete this tree's three-season cycle of beauty.

SOIL: Deep, rich, acidic, moist

LIGHT: Full sun or light shade

HARDINESS: Zone 5

COMMENTS: Although this tree needs room, place it where you can appreciate the flowers up close, because they are not noticeable from a distance. Also, try not to place the tree in a windy spot, because strong winds can greatly damage its symmetry.

WEEPING WILLOW
Salix babylonica

The weeping willow is one of the most strikingly beautiful trees for the landscape, provided it can be given room to develop and spread out properly. Its branches turn bright green early in the spring, with very long leaves that eventually turn olive green by summer. The 6-inch-long foliage and the pendulous branches give the tree its weeping effect. Leaves turn golden in the fall. The tree can grow 30 to 50 feet tall and equally wide.

SOIL: Any moist soil

LIGHT: Sun or part shade

HARDINESS: Zone 6

COMMENTS: Weeping willows should be placed where they will not interfere with other plants or structures. Their love of water often sends their roots into sewers and water pipes, causing serious problems. Avoid windy spots, because the branches break easily.

How to Plant a Tree

Trees can be planted any time the ground can be worked, but spring and fall are the best times to plant most types. If you plant in summer, you'll have to water more frequently. Spring planting is recommended for the rain tree, tulip tree, magnolia, black gum, and several oaks (red, scarlet, English, bur, willow, and white), which should not be moved in fall.

PLACEMENT

■ Because most trees need sun, plant a new specimen where it will not be shaded by buildings or larger trees. Consider the tree's mature size and shape, and don't locate it where it will eventually grow into other plants or your home.

Large shade trees with wide-spreading branches—such as oak, maple, linden, and elm—need at least 65 feet between their trunks. Plant them 30 feet from your house and 10 feet from walks, driveways, and patios so roots will not encroach upon and crack paved foundations. Columnar trees—such as gray birch, white poplar, and Lombardy poplar—can be planted closer together. Place small trees about 10 feet apart and at least 8 feet from your house.

SOIL PREPARATION

■ Although trees vary in their soil preferences, most do best in well-drained soils. To improve soil, till or spade in organic matter and a source of phosphorus, such as superphosphate. Do not fertilize again for at least another year.

Look also at the existing grade or soil level. If it needs to be raised, do so before planting. Grade changes made after a tree starts to grow can smother the roots and eventually damage or even kill the tree.

1 To plant balled-and-burlapped stock, first dig a hole twice as wide and at least 1½ times as deep as the root ball of the tree. This will allow for future root growth and avoid root damage.

TYPES OF TREE STOCK

■ Trees are sold as bare root, balled-and-burlapped, or containerized. Planting instructions for trees that are balled-and-burlapped are outlined in steps 1 through 6 on the *opposite* page. Follow the same steps for containerized material, but remove the container before planting. For all types, if you must delay planting time, keep the tree in a cool, shaded area, and water well until it can be set into the ground.

Plant bare-root trees in spring or fall when they are dormant. Keep the roots moist until planting, and soak roots in a bucket of water for 24 hours before planting. Form a cone of improved soil in the bottom of the planting hole and spread roots evenly over the cone. Remove broken or damaged roots and shorten too-long roots that would end up encircling the hole and competing with neighboring roots. Then follow steps 4 through 6 as outlined *opposite* for planting balled-and-burlapped trees.

POST-PLANTING CARE

■ Prune a newly planted tree to compensate for any root loss. Pruning a young tree helps develop its ultimate shape, size, and strength.

Newly planted trees should be staked to give them strength against high winds. Trees under 1 inch across

2 Place improved soil into the bottom of the hole so that the top of the ball will be level with the ground. Position the tree so its best side faces forward.

3 Cut the cord holding the ball and gently pull back, but do not remove, the burlap. That way, the root ball will not be disturbed. In time, the burlap will disintegrate.

4 Backfill the planting hole with improved soil until it is about half full, and water again. Tamp down the soil, holding the tree in a straight, upright position.

do not require staking. For trees with trunks between 1 and 3 inches across, use two stakes; trunks over 3 inches thick need support from three evenly placed stakes. Stakes should be tall enough to secure the tree just below the spot where the major branches split away from the trunk. Tie trees with heavy cord to prevent injury to bark. Don't wrap wire directly around bark.

Young trees, clad only in thin bark, are susceptible to sunscald. This malady occurs when the bark of the tree is warmed during the day by the winter sun, then is suddenly subjected to freezing temperatures at night. This condition often weakens trees. To prevent sunscald, wrap trees with a long strip of burlap or tree tape. Keep this protection in place until the tree develops the thick bark that mature trees have.

5 Fill the planting hole with water and allow it to drain. This will eliminate air pockets and ensure that roots will be in contact with soil particles.

6 After the water has drained, fill the planting hole to the top with improved soil. Make a catch basin for water by creating a raised circle of soil 2 to 3 inches high about a foot away from the tree.

CARE AND MAINTENANCE

Keep your prized shade trees healthy by paying attention to fertilizing, watering, winter protection, and insect and disease control.

FEEDING METHODS
■ Large trees should be fed every 3 to 4 years. Feeding in early spring or late fall is preferable; use a complete fertilizer such as 10-6-4 for trees that do not flower, or 5-10-5 for the ones that do.

To feed trees, either broadcast fertilizer on the soil surface, or inject it directly into the root zone. Trees in a lawn area can be surface-fed by applying fertilizer at a distance of 2½ feet from the trunk to 2 to 3 feet beyond the spread of the tree's branches. Use 10-6-4 at a rate of 1 pound per inch of trunk diameter for trees 3 inches across or less, and 3 pounds per inch of trunk diameter for trees over 3 inches across.

You can use a crowbar or a root feeder to make holes for feeding. For either method, fertilizer should be applied at least 2 feet from the base of the trunk. Feeder roots of younger trees are just inside the drip line (at the farthest tip of branches), and those of mature trees are outside the drip line.

For the crowbar method, make holes with a crowbar or auger at the rate of 10 to 15 for each inch of trunk diameter; space holes evenly around the perimeter of the drip line. Feed at the rate of 3 to 4 pounds of fertilizer per inch of trunk diameter if the tree's diameter is more than 6 inches, and 2 to 3 pounds per inch of diameter if it's less than 6 inches. Mix fertilizer with soil and pour into hole; do not use more than one cup of fertilizer per hole. Water well.

To make the feeding process even easier, use a root feeder (*right*). Simply fill the chamber with a compressed plant food cartridge, attach a garden hose to the feeder, and turn on the water. These feeders can also be used for deep-watering tree roots during periods of drought in the summer.

WATERING
■ Evergreens need special attention before cold weather settles in. Because these plants retain their foliage, they're very vulnerable to drying winter winds. Those on the south and west sides of your house will be the first to suffer. Unless you've had an especially wet fall, water all evergreens deeply before the ground freezes.

DISEASE AND INSECTS
■ Be on the lookout for signs of insects and diseases and treat them immediately. A dormant oil spray applied just before buds break will control many insect problems; do not apply dormant oil to sensitive plants such as sugar and Japanese maple, beech, hickory, walnut, butternut, Atlantic cedar, blue spruce, or Douglas fir.

INJURY REPAIR

■ If a large piece of bark is knocked off, nail it back before it dries out and cover the area with damp peat moss held in place with plastic, until the bark regrows. Or cut away the damaged bark and shape the wound into an oval with a sharp knife. Cover the area with a tree wound paint and inspect regularly. If the paint breaks or wears away, reapply.

Trees that have been damaged by the wind can usually be repaired. If young trees start to tilt from heavy winds, bring them back to their normal upright position and hold in place with wires or stakes until they strengthen and start to grow on their own. Uprooted trees may be saved if they are immediately righted and staked. Compensate for root loss by thinning out branches or pruning back.

Prune evergreens to maintain a pleasing, natural shape. This upright juniper should be trimmed back with hedge clippers to keep its pyramidal form.

This pine should be encouraged to retain a rounder shape. To keep branches compact and dense, cut the new growth (called a candle) back about halfway each spring.

Apply a sturdy plastic tree wrap to young trees to prevent damage to the bark from mowers and animals. This type of wrap is especially good for preventing rabbits from making a meal of your young trees.

Wrapping young trees can prevent sunscalding. In the fall, tie a tree wrap from the bottom up so there will be no lip that can collect water and cause fungus cankers to develop on the trunk.

Sometimes a leader will fail to grow or will break off. Select a shoot to be the new leader, and cut the surrounding ones back. If necessary, guide the leader into an upright position with a small stake.

SHRUBS IN THE LANDSCAPE

Shrubs can put the finishing touches on an existing planting scheme, serve as a first budget-minded purchase for a new home, or rejuvenate a tired landscape. Before making your selections, consider your special situation and the shrubs that will grow best in your climate.

TYPES OF SHRUBS
■ Shrubs fall into three general categories: (1) Narrow-leaved, or coniferous, evergreens, which keep their foliage year-round. Many are pyramidal in shape. Pines, yews, and junipers belong to this group. (2) Broad-leaved evergreens, including rhododendrons, hollies, boxwoods, and camellias. Some are evergreen only in the South. (3) Deciduous shrubs, which lose their leaves once a year. Many are flowering.

HOW TO SELECT SHRUBS
■ The shrubs you choose should blend with, not detract from, the style of your house. If you have a ranch-style house, for example, avoid shrubs that will grow up to block windows, and plants with severe upright forms that conflict with the house's horizontal lines.

To create a natural setting for your home, use shrubs to soften structural edges. Informal masses of evergreens at the corners of a two-story house, for example, will produce a lush frame around its foundation. For best effect, use shrubs with contrasting size and texture. The feathery foliage of juniper will enhance the looks of a shiny broad-leaved evergreen.

Although shrubs are usually planted in groups, some types can stand on their own. These specimens should have something special to offer, such as flowers, unique shape, or colorful foliage.

In the front yard *below,* a variety of evergreen shrubs and trees planted along the house and driveway add beauty and privacy. Consider the ultimate plant heights so your shrubs won't outgrow their setting.

For a showy, gracefully arching accent, try weigela (*right*). This deciduous shrub is tolerant of most soil types and prefers full sun or partial shade. Blossom colors are white, pink, red, and magenta.

SHRUBS IN THE LANDSCAPE

In southern gardens, few shrubs can compare with the bold and beautiful hibiscus. Growing to a height of 15 feet, this compact, hardy shrub looks best near an entryway, planted as a specimen, or mixed with lower-growing flowers. In the narrow bed at *right,* Agnes Galt hibiscus blooms with red- and pink-flowering snapdragons, petunias, and geraniums. Hibiscus grows best in a sunny location and is available in both red- and white-flowering varieties. Some hibiscus varieties are hardy in northern states.

Although full sun is best, the following shrubs will tolerate light shade: rhododendron, honeysuckle, hydrangea, aucuba, andromeda, mahonia, mountain laurel, winged euonymus, kerria, sweet pepperbush, and rose-of-Sharon.

The broad-leaved evergreens are the aristocrats of the evergreen family. Hardy only in areas where winter temperatures stay above zero, these shrubs have glossy green foliage that contrasts beautifully with their hardier needle-leaved cousins. Many species, including rhododendron, oleander, and andromeda, also produce dazzling flowers.

The lily-of-the-valley-like flowers of andromeda (*right*) appear every spring. You can use andromeda in a foundation planting or as a specimen plant. Andromeda prefers a moist, partially shady location with slightly acidic soil. Of the two most popular species, floribunda and japonica, the floribunda is slightly more hardy. Although it's slow growing, andromeda will eventually reach a height of 15 feet if left unpruned. If pruning is required, do it right after the flowers fade.

Use deciduous flowering shrubs as a colorful and less-demanding alternative to annual and perennial flowers. In just a few years, the lilacs at *left* transformed a bare, unsightly garden spot into a pocket of brilliance. One lavender- and one white-flowering variety mark the beginning of this border filled with hostas and coralbells.

The lilac's large, fragrant heads of single or double flowers make it a garden treasure during the months of May and June. This popular shrub grows to about 12 feet tall but can be pruned to any height to make a specimen plant or hedge. Available in shades of purple, blue, white, and pink, the lilac thrives in a sunny location with a slightly alkaline soil. Only dense shade prevents this hardy plant from blooming.

Because shrub borders are permanent landscape features, select shrubs that will provide interest year-round. Colorful berries, bark, and foliage will carry on the show long after spring blooms have faded. The low-growing *Viburnum plicatum* at *left* has showy, maplelike leaves and produces crownlike heads of small white flowers in May. In fall, its leaves turn scarlet, and red berries hang from the plant's branches even after the leaves have fallen off.

Other shrubs that provide brilliant fall foliage color include sumac, rhododendron, crape myrtle, and mahonia. For berries, try pyracantha, cotoneaster, holly, quince, chokeberry, bayberry, barberry, and mahonia. Shrubs with beautiful bare branches for winter landscapes include red-osier dogwood, chokeberry, kerria, crape myrtle, witch hazel, and sumac.

GALLERY OF SHRUBS

AZALEA
Rhododendron species and varieties

All azaleas are rhododendrons, but not all rhododendrons are azaleas. The difference, technically, is that azaleas have 5 stamens; rhododendrons have 10. Azaleas generally are shorter, with smaller leaves and flowers. Colors range from white through pink, red, orange, salmon, yellow, and purple. Many azaleas also are deciduous.
SOIL: Rich, moist, and acidic
LIGHT: Azaleas can take full sun or light shade.
HARDINESS: Zone 4 to 6
COMMENTS: Try Sweet, Flame, Ghent, Indica, Hiryu, Snow, Pinxterbloom, Roseshell, Rosebud, Royal, Swamp, or Pinkshell azaleas, or the Exbury, Knap Hill, Mollis, Indian, Kurume, or Gable hybrids. These plants do best in cooler climates and should always be mulched to keep roots cool. Be careful when cultivating azaleas not to disturb the roots.

BARBERRY
Berberis species

Barberries are thorny shrubs, with yellow flowers and black, red, yellow, or blue berries. Plants generally reach about 6 feet tall. Leaves are mostly glossy green, but some types within the Japanese barberries have red foliage. Depending on the type, barberries can be either deciduous or evergreen.
SOIL: Any soil, even poor and dry, for deciduous; moist and rich for evergreen types.
LIGHT: Full sun or part shade
HARDINESS: Zone 5 to 6
COMMENTS: Barberries are one of the best shrubs for hedges. The thorns also make them good barrier plants. The best types—those that are also immune to black stem rust—are evergreen Magellan, Wintergreen (*Berberis julianae*), Mentor or Warty (*B. verruculosa*); and deciduous Japanese (*B. thunbergi*) and Korean.

BOXWOOD
Buxus species

There are two types of boxwood grown in this country: common or English box (*Buxus sempervirens*) and Japanese or littleleaf box (*B. microphylla*). Both are excellent hedge plants, with small, glossy green leaves. Common box is taller, reaching up to 20 feet high, and littleleaf box reaches only 3 feet tall.
SOIL: Rich, moist, well drained
LIGHT: Full sun or light shade
HARDINESS: Common box, Zone 6; littleleaf, Zone 7
COMMENTS: Boxwood is the classic hedging material from English or Colonial gardens. It takes well to shearing; leaves and stems are soft and graceful. Within the littleleaf box, try *B. microphylla koreana*. There are Korean, compacta and japonica varieties. Within the common box, a number of choices include Angustifolia, Suffruticosa, and the variety Argenteo-variegata with white-spotted leaves. In northern areas, protect from winter winds with burlap.

BROOM, SCOTCH
Cytisus scoparius

The name comes from an old-time custom of using this plant to make brooms for sweeping floors. Scotch broom is a fast-growing, 4- to 6-foot shrub with upright or trailing bright green branches and masses of bright yellow, pealike flowers in mid-spring.

SOIL: Prefers acidic, dry soil that is not too fertile.
LIGHT: Full sun
HARDINESS: Zone 6
COMMENTS: Broom is an excellent addition to the formal garden or naturalized setting. It also adds interest to winter landscapes because the branches retain their bright green color all year. To keep plants compact, prune after flowering. Brooms are hard to transplant, so choose sites carefully to avoid having to move them later.

CAMELLIA
Camellia japonica or *C. sasanqua*

These broad-leaved evergreens rank among the most beautiful of garden shrubs. The more common *C. japonica* is a shrub or small tree with 4-inch glossy leaves. It produces large, waxy white, pink, or red flowers in late winter or early spring. The *C. sasanqua* is smaller in all respects, blooming in winter in mild areas.

SOIL: Rich, acidic, moist
LIGHT: Partial shade
HARDINESS: *C. japonica,* Zone 7; *C. sasanqua,* Zone 8
COMMENTS: Camellias are fairly easy to grow. However, camellia buds may freeze in borderline areas. Use a light winter protection in these areas. Pruning is generally not necessary.

There are many varieties of camellias to choose from, including those with single, semi-double, and double flowers that resemble roses or peonies.

CEANOTHUS (wild lilac)
Ceanothus species

This large family of evergreens includes small trees, shrubs, and ground covers that—depending on species—grow wild from the eastern United States to California. Flowers that bloom in early spring range from white through tones of blue to purple. The flowers are shaped like tiny lilacs in a pyramidal form.

SOIL: Poor, dry soil is best to discourage root rot. Ceanothus is extremely drought resistant.
LIGHT: Full sun
HARDINESS: Zone 5 to 9
COMMENTS: Many of the native varieties are named for the areas in which they were found; for example, San Diego, Point Reyes, Carmel, Santa Barbara, and Mt. Tranquillon. Other good varieties are Feltleaf, Floire de Versailles, and Blue Blossom.

GALLERY OF SHRUBS

CRANBERRY, HIGHBUSH
Viburnum trilobum

As with all viburnums, the highbush cranberry is a decorative addition to the garden. Flat flower clusters are 2 to 4 inches across, with a small group of flowers in the center and a margin of large flowers rimming the outside. Blooms are white, followed by red cranberrylike berries that start in mid-summer and continue through winter. Plants grow to 12 feet, with lobed, maplelike leaves that turn red in fall.
SOIL: Average, well drained
LIGHT: Full sun or part shade
HARDINESS: Zone 3
COMMENTS: In the garden, highbush cranberry serves as a decorative hedge, screen planting, or specimen, requiring little pruning. Beyond that, the berries are edible and good in jams and jellies. This plant does best in the north, because it likes a cold dormant period. A compact variety reaches only 5 feet.

DOGWOOD
Cornus species

This family of shrubs and small trees contains some of the best landscape plants available. All are known for spring flowers, fall berries, and a spectacular autumn color. Dogwood will fare well anywhere except where the summers are extremely hot and dry. The Siberian or tatarian dogwood (*C. alba*) has white flowers in spring followed by light blue berries, and vivid red twigs all winter. The red-osier (*C. sericea*) has white fruits and flowers. This species has a variety called Flaviramea, with yellow twigs. The Cornelian cherry (*C. mas*) is covered with a cloud of yellow flowers in very early spring. It can reach 24 feet in height; the others grow to 10 feet.
SOIL: Rich, moist
LIGHT: Full sun or part shade
HARDINESS: Zone 3 to 5
COMMENTS: Prune those with colored twigs often to force new, more highly colored growth.

EUONYMUS, WINGED
Burning bush (*Euonymus alata*)

This shrub gets its two common names from two distinct characteristics. The stems of the plant are encased in a stiff, corky covering that looks like wings. In fall, the foliage color is so brilliant that the plant appears to be on fire. Plants generally grow 7 to 10 feet tall, except for the variety Compacta which reaches 4 to 6 feet. The stems are rigid, in a vaselike shape, and particularly decorative after the leaves fall. Flowers are inconspicuous.
SOIL: Not fussy about soil.
LIGHT: Full sun to heavy shade
HARDINESS: Zone 4
COMMENTS: The winged euonymus makes an excellent hedge, with very little pruning required. The stems also make interesting material for arrangements. A close relative is the evergreen euonymus (*E. japonica*), with green or variegated foliage.

FORSYTHIA
Forsythia x intermedia

A true harbinger of spring, the forsythia usually is the first shrub to bloom, with yellow-gold flowers appearing before the leaves. Blooms are single, up to 2 inches long, with a trumpet shape. Branches are stiff, yet slightly arching to fountain shape. Foliage is medium to deep green. Fast-growing, forsythia reaches a height of 8 to 10 feet.
SOIL: Any type
LIGHT: Full sun or light shade
HARDINESS: Zone 5
COMMENTS: Forsythia is useful as a specimen plant and in hedges, screens, or borders. Bring an early spring into your house by cutting off several branches and forcing them into early bloom. Good varieties include: Beatrix Farrand, Lynwood Gold, Spectabilis, Spring Glory, and Arnold Dwarf. Other good species are *F. suspensa* (weeping) and *F. ovata* (Korean).

HOLLY
Ilex species

The holly group covers a large number of evergreen and deciduous small trees and shrubs. Flowers are inconspicuous, but the black or red berries are most decorative in fall and winter. All but the Chinese holly require both male and female plants to produce berries.
SOIL: Well drained, slightly acidic
LIGHT: Full sun to part shade
HARDINESS: Zone 4 to 7
COMMENTS: Least hardy: English (*I. aquifolium*), with blue-black grapelike fruits and bronze fall leaves; and Chinese (*I. cornuta*), with red berries. Midzone: Japanese (*I. crenata*), with black berries; Long-stalk (*I. pedunculosa*), with red, drooping berries and spineless leaves; and American (*I. opaca*) a columnar, evergreen tree with short, spreading branches. Hardy: Gallberry (*I. glabra*), with white flowers and black berries; and Winterberry (*I. verticillata*) with red berries and dull leaves.

HONEYSUCKLE
Lonicera tatarica

A favorite in northern climates, the honeysuckle is an upright-growing, dense, twiggy plant that reaches 8 to 10 feet in height. Its vigorous growth makes it ideal for screening and hedging. Very tiny flowers of pale pink or red in mid-spring create a flush of color over blue-green leaves. In early summer, miniature-size berries of red form and last until eaten by the birds.
SOIL: Any type
LIGHT: Full sun to part shade. The growth is less dense in shade.
HARDINESS: Zone 4
COMMENTS: Although relatively disease- and insect-free, honeysuckles require very frequent pruning to thin out twiggy branches. Popular varieties include Arnold Red, Grandiflora, Alba, Modern Orange, Virginalis, Rosea, Sibirica, Zabeli.

GALLERY OF SHRUBS

JUNIPER
Juniperus species

Name a plant shape and there's a juniper that conforms to it, from a low ground cover to a tall tree. All are serviceable landscape plants, with interesting foliage that is both scaly and needlelike—sometimes on the same plant. There are variegated forms in silver and gold and in blue-greens. All are tough and sturdy, needing minimal care.

SOIL: Dry, sandy, light
LIGHT: Full sun preferred
HARDINESS: Zone 3 to 7
COMMENTS: Best known varieties are Japanese (*J. chinensis*) and its variety Pfitzer, a broad horizontal; Common (*J. communis stricta*), a tall, narrow plant; Shore (*J. conferta*), a soft ground cover; *J. horizontalis* varieties including Bar Harbor and Blue Rug, mounding ground covers; and *J. h. plumosa*, including Andorra, a spreading, loose plant. Junipers love heat, but may redden in winter. They all prune well.

KERRIA
Kerria japonica

Kerria is available in both single- and double-flowering varieties, but the double form clearly makes the superior plant. In mid-spring, the plant is clothed with a multitude of golden yellow blooms about 1½ inches across. The double flowers, sometimes called globe flowers, are densely petaled and ball-like. The slightly arching branches remain bright green all winter long. Leaves are triangular, serrated, and 2 to 4 inches long, turning yellow before falling in autumn. Kerria is 4 to 6 feet tall at maturity.

SOIL: Average
LIGHT: Part shade; full sun in areas where it remains cool.
HARDINESS: Zone 4
COMMENTS: Kerria tends to spawn suckers easily, losing its shrublike appearance. Keep pruned to shape.

LILAC
Syringa vulgaris and hybrids

From mid-spring to early summer—depending on the variety—lilacs fill a garden with their legendary fragrance and flowers. Lilac flowers grow in large, cone-shape clusters of small blooms that range in color from blue to light and deep purple, to pink, to white. Lilacs grow 10 to 12 feet tall and have heart-shape leaves.

SOIL: Well drained and fertilized
LIGHT: Full sun
HARDINESS: Zone 4. Does best where winters are cold.
COMMENTS: To maintain healthy, vigorous growth, plant them where they'll get good air circulation. To maximize blooms—which often do well only every other year—keep soil limy and fertile. Remove seed clusters and dead flowers. Remove suckers, leaving some to keep plant bushy. Of the hundreds of varieties to choose from, the French hybrids are generally regarded as the best.

OLEANDER
Nerium oleander

Where hot, dry, desert conditions exist, the oleander is a shrub of choice. Evergreen oleander, with its long, narrow leaves, grows rapidly to 10 to 12 feet high and as wide around. Blooms are 2 to 3 inches wide in tones of pink, coral, red, white, or yellow. Flowers start to appear in early spring and last throughout the summer months. Many varieties of oleander are fragrant.

SOIL: Any soil. Oleander is heat-, drought-, and salt-tolerant.
LIGHT: Full sun
HARDINESS: Zone 9
COMMENTS: The cool appearance of the oleander in a hot, dry spot is a refreshing sight. To keep the plant blooming each spring, remove the branches that bloomed the previous year. Be careful when you discard branches and leaves, because they are poisonous. Watch out for insect and disease problems prevalent in oleander.

PRUNUS (flowering almond)
Prunus triloba

A refreshing breath of pale pink covers the branches of this shrub during early spring before the leaves begin to develop. Flowers are small (about 1 inch across) and double; no fruits form. The flowering almond generally stays about 6 feet high (although it can get taller) and quite rounded.

SOIL: Average
LIGHT: Full sun or light shade
HARDINESS: Zone 5
COMMENTS: A number of cousins to the flowering almond deserve a place in the landscape. The beach plum (*P. maritima*) is a favorite at the seashore because of its hardiness and tolerance to salt spray. Flowers are white and fruits are delicious. The Nanking cherry (*P. tomentosa*) makes a marvelous hedge, with tiny white flowers in early spring and delicious red berries in summer. Nanking cherry is the hardiest member of the prunus species.

RHODODENDRON
Rhododendron species

Rhododendron is a class of mostly large—to 12 feet—shrubs with dark green, elongated leaves and colorful trusses of flowers that stand proudly above the foliage in mid- to late spring and early summer. Blooms can be red, purple, white, or pink.

SOIL: Rich, moist, acidic
LIGHT: Part shade
HARDINESS: Zone 4 to 6
COMMENTS: For best results, remove flower heads after blooming and keep roots well mulched. Most popular types are: Carolina (*R. carolinianum*), a compact plant with rust-colored leaf undersides; p.j.m., a hybrid, low grower with purple blooms; Catawba (*R. catawbiense*), the source of many of today's hybrids; Rosebay (*R. maximum*), the largest of the group; and *R. impeditum*, a dwarf, rock garden plant with small, almost blue flowers in early spring.

GALLERY OF SHRUBS

SPIREA
Spiraea species

Arching branches are covered in mid-spring with rounded clusters of tiny flowers to make this shrub a white fountain of bloom. Plants reach 6 to 8 feet in height, and spread equally wide. Give spirea room to show off its attractive shape. Branches are numerous and thin, and filled with small, round, scalloped leaves of bluish green. Easy to care for, spirea is an excellent choice for hedges or as a border plant.
SOIL: Average
LIGHT: Full sun or part shade
HARDINESS: Zone 5
COMMENTS: In addition to this spirea, there are several others used in the landscape. Thunberg (*S. thunbergi*) blooms earlier in spring, with single white flowers along the stem; the plant has a more upright habit. Japanese (*S. japonica*) and Anthony Waterer (*S. bumalda*) are summer-blooming, low-growing, pink-flowered shrubs.

VIBURNUM
Viburnum species

If you have a window view you enjoy in spring, be sure to plant a viburnum nearby. Edged in pink, the white flowers grow in clusters and are deliciously fragrant; many look like snowballs and carry that term as a common name. Most form berries in fall in bright shades of red, blue, black, or yellow. All are easy to grow, with few pests. Many have a red or scarlet fall color.
SOIL: Moist, well drained, acidic
LIGHT: Full sun
HARDINESS: Zone 5 to 6
COMMENTS: The best viburnums are: Tea (*V. setigerum*), the only one with bright orange berries; Double File (*V. plicatum tomentosum*), with stiff horizontal branches; Leatherleaf (*V. rhytidophyllum*), with very rough leaves that are evergreen in Zone 7 and warmer; Fragrant (*V. carlesi*); Siebold (*V. sieboldi*); and Linden (*V. dilatatum*).

WEIGELA
Weigela florida

The weigela has been delighting gardeners for years. It's known for its display of color from late spring to early summer. Blooms are funnel-shape, in shades of red, white, or pink. Some open in a light color and darken as they mature; others are two-toned or bicolored in very bright tones. Branches are arching, and covered with green or variegated foliage. Plants grow to 6 to 10 feet, although several dwarf varieties are also available.
SOIL: Average
LIGHT: Full sun or part shade
HARDINESS: Zone 6
COMMENTS: Weigela is essentially a pest-free plant, but it isn't particularly attractive when not in bloom. It needs to be pruned carefully and frequently, because a lot of winter damage can occur. Recommended varieties include Bristol Ruby, Bristol Snowflake, Variegata, and Newport Red. *W. maximowiczi* has greenish yellow blooms.

WILLOW, PUSSY
Salix discolor

The inch-long, soft, silky, fuzzy, gray catkins that appear in very early spring are the main attraction of this large shrub or small tree. The catkins are often cut and forced for early bouquets. Colorful bright yellow stamens appear only on male plants. Pussy willows break open at the end of their cycle, spreading seed around the garden. The plant can grow to 20 feet tall. New branches are red-brown, so frequent pruning produces more of these instead of the mature gray branches. The pussy willow is fast growing and can become unsightly if not kept in bounds.
SOIL: Poor, moist soil is best.
LIGHT: Sun or shade
HARDINESS: Zone 3
COMMENTS: A smaller, more attractive pussy willow is Rose Gold (*S. gracilistyla*). Catkins are rose and gold toned, but the plant is less hardy.

WITCH HAZEL
Hamamelis species

Witch hazels are treasured for their very fragrant, unusually shaped flowers that appear in late fall or late winter. The flowers look like masses of thin ribbons or strings, in a golden yellow color. Under unseasonably cold conditions, the flowers protect themselves by closing into a tight ball.
SOIL: Rich, moist, well drained
LIGHT: Sun or light shade
HARDINESS: Zone 5 to 6
COMMENTS: Common (*H. virginiana*)—the hardiest and largest (to 25 feet) fall-flowering variety—has medium-sized blooms that blend with yellow fall foliage. Vernal (*H. vernalis*)—smallest, most rounded shape (6 feet high and wide)—has the smallest (½-inch) flowers in late winter. Chinese (*H. mollis*)—largest plant with the largest spring flowers—is prone to cold damage. Arnold Promise (*H. x intermedia*) is showiest with red fall color.

YEW
Taxus species

If you need a trouble-free conifer for your landscape, the yew is one of the best plants to choose. Its dark green, 1-inch needles are complemented by red berries in midsummer. Desirable for year-round landscape use because of its evergreen nature and its growth habits, yews fall into two basic groups: English (*T. baccata*) and Japanese (*T. cuspidata*). *T. x media* is a cross between the two. Yews can be found in a number of shapes, including globe, vase, columnar, pyramidal, or ground hugging.
SOIL: Average, well drained with no wet feet
LIGHT: Sun or shade
HARDINESS: English, Zone 6
Japanese, Zone 5
COMMENTS: Recommended varieties include the upright (*T. c. capitata*); Spreading English (*T.b. repandens*); and Hicks (*T. media hicksi*).

HOW TO PLANT A SHRUB

Spring and fall are the best times to plant new shrubs. Many gardeners prefer fall planting, because shrub roots will grow well into winter, giving the plant a head start on top growth the following spring.

The old adage about not putting a $10 plant in a 10-cent hole still holds true, and it's one to be adhered to if you want shrubs to perform in your landscape. Before digging a hole, consider your shrub's needs, including sunlight, soil conditions, pruning requirements, and winter protection.

SOIL PREPARATION
■ Loose, fertile soil will provide adequate drainage and aeration and retain water and nutrients to sustain plant growth. You may need to improve your shrub's soil. Before planting, test the soil for its pH level. Most shrubs require a neutral pH (between 6 and 7). If you have a low (too acidic) pH, add a phosphorus source, such as superphosphate or lime. Some broad-leaved evergreens, such as rhododendrons and azaleas, prefer an acidic soil. If your soil's pH is too high, you can lower it by mixing in sulfur or iron sulfate.

TYPES OF SHRUB STOCK
■ Shrubs are sold in one of three ways: bare root, the type usually sold by mail-order nurseries; balled-and-burlapped (B&B), almost always an evergreen which is field grown, dug with a ball of soil around its roots, and wrapped in burlap; and container grown, most often used for deciduous stock.

Timing is important when planting shrubs. Bare-root or deciduous shrubs should be planted when they're dormant, either in early spring before growth starts or in late fall after it has stopped. Container and balled-and-burlapped plants are most successfully planted when temperatures are cool and root growth is at its height, but they can be planted at any time the soil is workable. In the summer, give extra attention to watering.

BARE-ROOT SHRUBS
■ Bare-root shrubs should be planted as soon as possible. If planting is delayed, keep roots cool and moist by wrapping them in dampened peat moss or newspaper. To plant the shrub, dig a hole that will accommodate all of the shrub's roots. Never crowd the roots or jam

Remove containers by turning them upside down and tapping them gently or by cutting them away with shears. If roots are encircled around the ball, be sure to loosen them before planting.

When you plant B&B shrubs, set the plant at the same level it grew before. Remove any wires or cords. Pull the burlap slightly away from the ball, but do not remove it; it will disintegrate in time.

them into the bottom of a hole that's too small. After digging the hole, mold a loose cone of soil in the bottom. Set the shrub on top of the cone and spread the roots over it. Holding the shrub in an upright position, fill the planting hole about two-thirds full. Gently tamp down the soil around the roots and fill the hole with water. After the water has drained, fill with soil.

BALLED-AND-BURLAPPED AND CONTAINER SHRUBS

■ Balled-and-burlapped and container-grown shrubs are more expensive than bare-root plants. Because they're already growing in their root balls, however, they'll adjust more quickly to transplanting and start growing much

faster. Both of these types must be kept well watered until planted. At planting time, dig a hole larger than the root ball. Set the shrub into the hole at the same level it grew before. Loosen the burlap only at the trunk. (The burlap will decay rapidly and will not interfere with root development.) If the root ball is wrapped in a plastic or cardboard container, carefully cut away the covering after the shrub is positioned in the hole. Backfill the hole as you would with a bare-root shrub.

POST-PLANTING CARE

■ To help a deciduous shrub adjust to the shock of transplanting, remove about one-third of the branches. Pruning will compensate for any possible

root loss during the move. Start by cutting out broken branches and young shoots sprouting low on the plant. Then cut away the weaker branch of any V-shaped crotch. Shear evergreens only to make the shape of the plant uniform.

Top priority should be given to watering newly planted shrubs. Dig a shallow trough around the root area to catch water. If rainfall is low the first season, saturate the soil at least once a week with a light trickle from a garden hose, or use a soaker hose.

Mulch will help conserve moisture, ward off weeds, and keep soil insulated in the winter. Place a 3- to 4-inch layer of straw, wood chips, or leaves beneath the spread of branches to within an inch or two of the trunk.

CARE AND MAINTENANCE

Shrubs are among the easiest plants to care for. Except for pruning, you'll need to spend a minimal amount of time to keep them at their best.

FERTILIZING

■ Evergreen shrubs will grow without fertilizing, but deciduous shrubs benefit from a supplementary feeding once a year. The best times to feed are early spring or late fall after the plants have gone dormant. Fertilizing in late fall is often more beneficial because it allows the roots to take up nutrients in the very early spring when root growth starts. Don't feed shrubs in late summer or early fall, because feeding stimulates new growth that will not have time to harden off before winter's cold.

Use a complete fertilizer containing 5 to 12 percent nitrogen. For flowering shrubs, a fertilizer rich in phosphorus (such as 5-10-5) is best. Feed nonflowering shrubs at the same time you feed the lawn, with the same fertilizer.

Apply fertilizer evenly to the soil area as far as the branches reach to cover the entire root zone; water well. A supplementary liquid fertilizer applied to the foliage and soil will give an extra boost. To avoid burning the leaves, do not spray them on hot, sunny days.

Broad-leaved evergreens, such as azalea, rhododendron, camellia, laurel, and leucothoe, require an acidic soil to keep growing and blooming. For best results, dust annually with cottonseed meal or a special rhododendron-azalea-camellia fertilizer.

WATERING AND WEEDING

■ Watering and weeding are the two essentials for shrub survival, especially for young plants. Mulch will help re-

duce many of the time-consuming maintenance chores by keeping the ground cool, moist, and weed-free. Do not lay mulch all the way to the shrub's stems; direct contact can cause stem rot, and organic material makes attractive nesting sites for small animals who may make a meal of your shrubs. During periods of hot, dry weather, water shrubs deeply on a weekly basis.

INSECTS AND DISEASES

■ Unfortunately, some insects and diseases like your shrubs as much as you do. For insurance against insect invasions, use a dormant oil spray on flowering shrubs in early spring before buds break. Such sprays can control scales, and often aphids and mites, on a variety of evergreen and deciduous plants. If your shrubs still show signs of stress, consult your local nurseryman.

Shrubs used as hedges should be cut back regularly to keep them in shape. Prune the bottom of the hedge wider than the top so the sun will fall on bottom branches and keep them full and dense.

Use the proper tools when caring for your shrubs. Sharp pruning shears should be used to head back evergreens or to train shrubs into special topiary or espalier shapes.

Use shears designed for each pruning job. Hedge clippers work well on thin or soft stems. For stems thicker than the center of pruning shears, use loppers or saw.

To increase next year's bloom on lilacs and rhododendrons, cut off this year's flower heads after blooming. Don't remove blossoms from fall berry producers.

Some shrubs, like forsythia, send out long arching branches. These can be rooted to form a new plant. Draw the stem to the ground and peg it down (left) with a clip to hold it in place until it roots.

WINTER PROTECTION

■ In cold-winter areas, protect marginally hardy deciduous plants with a thick mulch of leaves, evergreen boughs, or wood chips after frost. Remove the mulch in spring. Because evergreens retain their foliage, they are vulnerable to drying winter winds. Watering all evergreen shrubs deeply before the ground freezes will help. To provide further protection, set up a four-sided burlap screen, and fill the area between the screen and plant with leaves or straw. If snow or ice coats branches, remove it to prevent breakage.

ROSES IN THE LANDSCAPE

Every garden has room for at least one rosebush, if not more. In a shrub border, try mixing a few old-fashioned roses with spring-blooming plants like forsythia and lilac. As the flowers of the shrubs begin to fade, the roses will burst into bloom, extending the color show well into the summer.

MIXED OR ALONE

■ Perennial flowers and roses go well together, too. The roses provide continuous color while the various perennials go in and out of bloom. In the garden corner *below, right,* Olé, a fiery red grandiflora, blooms harmoniously alongside cranesbill geranium, sedum, snapdragon, lily, iris, statice, and delphinium. For perennial borders too small to accommodate the taller roses, you can add lots of color by edging the garden with miniature roses.

Climbers and ramblers are excellent for camouflaging unsightly buildings, fences, and walls. These vigorous plants grow rapidly and will completely cover the worst eyesore with blooms in just a season or two. Large, traditional rose arbors (*opposite*) are always impressive. Where space is tight, you can get the same effect with a modest arbor over your garden path. Sometimes just one climber in full bloom can be more effective than a whole border of flowers.

Roses provide a beautiful, fragrant border along a deck or patio. Choose white or light-colored roses if you use the patio at night, because they'll show up better in the dark.

Some roses will sprawl over the ground and act as a colorful ground cover. Similar types can be planted atop stone fences or retaining walls and allowed to spill to the ground.

Roses grown in containers are popular for small city gardens and balconies. Use compact minis and floribundas for best results. Move the pots around to create different effects.

HEDGE ROSES

■ A rose hedge will add elegance to your yard. Tall shrubs make excellent privacy screens. Medium-size floribundas divide property without giving that boxed-in look. Low-growing minis and polyanthas can separate areas with a bright strip of color.

When planting a hedge of roses, stick to one basic color and size, and space the plants closely together to ensure dense growth. If you're planting roses along a walkway or patio, set them far enough back so passersby will not be caught by thorns.

Mini-tree roses (*above*) bring a touch of elegance to your garden. These stately attention grabbers stand about 2 feet tall and look terrific set along a low garden wall.

ROSE CLASSIFICATION

Roses are classified into several categories based on a number of plant and blossom characteristics, including size, shape, and form. Classifications include the hybrid tea, floribunda, grandiflora, miniature, climber, old garden rose, shrub, and polyantha. A study of these rose classifications is a lesson in their history as well, from the oldest old garden rose, through a continuous series of developments and hybridizations, to present-day varieties.

The old garden rose class is divided into several subclasses, including alba, Bourbon, centifolia, China, Damask, Gallica, hybrid foetida, hybrid perpetual, hybrid spinosissima, moss, noisette, species, and tea. The shrub rose category includes eglanteria, hybrid moyesi, hybrid rugosa, kordesi, musk, and the shrub roses.

The grandiflora is a hybrid. From the hybrid tea, it inherits flower form and long cutting stems; from the floribunda, it receives hardiness and continuous clusters of bloom.

Any rose class existing before 1867 qualifies as an old garden rose. Old garden roses stand on their own virtues: hardiness, fragrance, and low maintenance.

As the buds of the hybrid tea open, they reveal swirls of petals and elegant, high-centered blooms on 2- to 5-foot-tall stems. Many emit the famous rose fragrance and are a perfect choice to fill a vase.

The floribunda is a cross between the classic hybrid tea and the polyantha, with its abundant sprays. Hardier and bushier than hybrid teas, floribundas make good landscape plants.

Few plants are as tough and tolerant of neglect and poor growing conditions as shrub roses. They vary in height from low-growing ground covers to taller types used in hedges.

ROSE CLASSIFICATION

Consider height, hardiness, and climatic needs when you select roses. Colors and forms should complement your landscape, as well as your taste.

THE AMERICAN ROSE SOCIETY

■ To make choosing roses easier, the American Rose Society, an international association of amateur and professional rose growers, has classified all roses into seventeen color categories: white, medium yellow, deep yellow, yellow blend, apricot blend, orange and orange blend, orange-red, light pink, medium pink, pink blend, medium red, dark red, red blend, mauve, russet, and mauve blend.

Each year, members of the American Rose Society establish ratings for commercially available rose varieties. This system gives a numerical rating from 0.0 to 10.0 for all roses. For a copy of these published ratings, send $1 to *Handbook for Selecting Roses*, Box 30000, Shreveport, LA 71130.

ALL-AMERICA ROSES

■ When choosing varieties for your rose garden, look also to the winners of the annual All-America Rose Selections (AARS) award. This organization, in existence since 1938, tests new roses to determine which are worthy of recommendation to American gardeners.

The AARS grows rose plants in over two dozen test gardens across the country so that each rose is exposed to a variety of soil and climatic conditions. Testing criteria include habit, vigor, hardiness, disease resistance, frequency of bloom, foliage, flower form, substance, opening and finishing color, fragrance, and novelty. After a two-year test, varieties with the highest scores receive the AARS highly acclaimed stamp of approval.

PERSONAL PREFERENCE

■ The final variety selection you make will depend on how you want to use the rose. If you want to plant a rose in a container, look for one that is compact and floriferous. A small container will best suit a miniature or a polyantha, and a larger container will accommodate one floribunda. For a hedge, choose a floribunda. Miniature roses are perfect for low edgings, and shrub roses work well for large screens. Along fences, try climbers, which also do well against arbors and trellises. Flower arranging enthusiasts should consider planting fragrant hybrid teas or grandifloras.

A miniature rose is a tiny reproduction of a full-size rose, with flowers, leaves, and stems shrunken in proportionate size. Plants range from 3 to 4 inches high to 18 to 24 inches tall.

Any bush rose variety can be grafted to an understock stem to create a tree rose. Tree roses can accent a bed, decorate a patio, or add distinction to any planting. They're ideal for a formal garden.

Climbers have long, pliable canes that can be trained on supports. These hardy plants produce loose clusters of large flowers. Climbing sports have the same flowers as their parents but are not as hardy.

HOW TO PLANT A ROSE

When should you plant roses? Bare-root roses should be planted at times when they are dormant and the ground is not frozen. In warm areas, this is in late winter. Where winter temperatures do not go below 0° Fahrenheit, planting may be done in early spring or late fall. In areas of extreme cold, roses should be planted only in the spring. Where possible, plant in fall, because roots will grow for much of the winter, leading to strong top growth in spring.

BARE-ROOT ROSES

■ Bare-root roses should be planted as soon as possible after you receive them. If you won't have a chance to plant them for several days, keep them in a cool, dark spot and keep the roots moist by wrapping them in damp newspaper or peat moss. If you can't plant your bare-root roses for several weeks, heel them in by burying the entire plant in a trench in a cool, shaded spot. Planting instructions for bare-root roses are outlined in steps 1 to 5 *opposite*.

CONTAINER ROSES

■ When you buy roses already growing in containers, you can extend the planting season into summer, allowing you to fill in bits of color in the garden where it's needed.

Plant container roses the same way as other containerized shrubs; be sure to carefully remove the container (*right*) before planting, to help ensure fast and strong root growth. Keep roses well-watered, especially in the summertime, until they're established.

PLACING AND SPACING

■ In most climates, hybrid teas, grandi-floras, and floribundas should be planted 24 inches apart. Where winters are mild, allow more space; for dense edging or hedging, space a little closer together. Because shrub and old garden roses will grow large, space them up to 4 to 6 feet apart, depending on their mature size. For climbers to be trained horizontally along a fence, allow a distance of 8 to 10 feet between plants. Plant minis from 8 to 18 inches apart depending on their mature size.

Plan ahead when placing roses in your landscape. Because they are permanent features, place them where they can remain indefinitely. Plant roses where they will receive at least 6 hours of direct sun each day; morning sun is preferable so the foliage can dry , which reduces the chances of disease. Where summer heat is intense, place roses where they will get light afternoon shade. Minis and climbers will be happy with a little less sun than their larger cousins, and can be grown in the shade of an ornamental tree. High winds can damage or destroy open flowers. If possible, protect roses from wind by planting by a fence, hedge, or other barrier.

GIVE ROSES A GOOD START

■ A rose is no better than the soil it's planted in, so give extra attention to soil preparation. Soil should be light and rich; improve it by mixing in organic matter such as peat moss, leaf mold, or compost. Heavy clay soils can be loosened with gypsum. Because roses don't like wet feet, improve soil drainage by adding perlite, vermiculite, or sand. The pH for roses should be between 6.0 and 6.5. Correct it with lime or sulfur if needed. Add superphosphate before planting.

KEEP RECORDS

■ A variety label is usually attached with a piece of wire to a cane on a rosebush. Insert the label into the ground near the rose, and keep a separate record of what varieties you plant.

1 Before planting, soak roots of bare-root roses in water overnight to restore lost moisture. Prune back any broken, damaged, or too-long roots.

2 Dig a hole 24 inches deep and wide, and place a mound of soil in the bottom of the hole. Position the bud union so that it is in line with ground level.

3 Backfill the planting hole two-thirds full, add water, and allow to drain. Fill the hole, then mound soil around the canes to keep them moist. Create a well around the mound and keep watered.

4 Roses can be further protected from drying out with a mulch of organic matter. Keep this in place until new growth begins, then wash away carefully with a gentle stream of water.

5 Prune roses back by a third after planting, and remove any dead or broken wood at the same time. This will encourage new, strong canes from the start.

CARE AND MAINTENANCE

If you take care of your roses, they will reward you all summer with beautiful blooms. Proper watering, mulching, fertilizing, and winter protection will help roses survive and flourish.

WATERING

■ With the right amount of water, roses will produce larger, longer-lasting blossoms with better color. One inch of water per week is ideal; use a rain gauge as a guide. During times of extended drought and high temperatures, water more frequently. Sandy soils may need to be watered more often and clay soils less often.

Roses can be watered by subirrigation pipes, soaker hoses laid on the ground, or overhead sprinklers. The method you choose will depend on your garden size and budget. Overhead sprinkling is one of the easiest and least expensive methods; water only in the morning so the leaves will not go through the night wet, which invites fungus problems.

MULCHING

■ In mid-spring, after the ground is warm, apply a 2- to 3-inch layer of mulch around your roses. In the summer, mulch will keep the soil cooler, moister, and more weed-free. As it decomposes, it also will enrich the soil. Left in place all winter, mulch will insulate the soil to help eliminate the threat of plants being heaved out of their resting places when the soil alternately freezes and thaws. Mulched roses will also stay cleaner because the protective covering prevents any soil from splattering the foliage and flowers during watering or rainstorms. Do not allow mulch to come in contact with canes.

Whether you're removing spent blossoms or cutting flowers for bouquets, make a cut at an angle above a 5-leaflet leaf, which is where the new growth will start.

Disbudding will give you one large flower per stem. Remove small buds as they appear around the central flower. On a floribunda, take out the center bud.

Roses should be fed three times a year with a rose fertilizer spread over the root area. Feed after pruning in early spring, just before the first bloom, and two months before the first expected fall frost.

Rose foliage needs regular spraying or dusting to prevent a variety of diseases, such as blackspot and mildew. Treat for aphids, Japanese beetles, and other insect problems as they appear.

WINTER PROTECTION

■ Most roses need protection in areas where winter temperatures regularly drop below 20 degrees Fahrenheit. Fluctuations in temperature, extended periods of severe cold, and harsh, drying winds cause winter dieback. A deep and constant snow cover can't be beat, but you'll probably need to provide additional protection. Shrub, old garden, and miniature roses, however, are relatively hardy and need little protection.

The best rosebush protection is to mound soil over canes to a height of at least 12 inches. Bring soil from another area to avoid exposing delicate feeder roots to cold air. Remove soil mound when growth starts in spring. For extra protection, mulch with wood chips or leaves. Apply mulch after the ground freezes, and carefully remove in spring.

1 Tree roses are particularly vulnerable to cold. They can be brought indoors, buried, or wrapped. To wrap, start by setting four stakes around the plant.

2 Wrap burlap around stakes and tie. This lets air circulate, lowers the chance of disease, and prevents premature growth caused by an interior greenhouse effect.

Where temperatures dip below zero, take climber canes off of supports and secure them on the ground. Cover with leaves or soil. You can also leave canes in place and wrap them with burlap.

Instead of using soil around canes, you can also mound up other organic materials, such as bark chips (*above*). In the spring, remove the material carefully to avoid breaking off new plant growth.

In very cold climates, rose plants need heavy protection. Use a paper, cardboard, plastic, or metal cylinder and fill it with bark, leaves, or newspaper. You can also use plastic foam rose cones.

INSECTS AND DISEASES

INSECT/DISEASE	DESCRIPTION AND TROUBLE SIGNS	CONTROL
Aphids	Aphids, also called plant lice, are tiny but visible green or brown insects that form colonies along flower buds and new shoot growth, starting in mid- to late spring. They harm roses by sucking away their vital juices.	Aphids can be knocked off the plant with a strong stream of water from the garden hose or with a spray of soapy water; or use a commercial insecticide.
Black spot	Black spot, as the name implies, is a fungus disease that causes rounded, black spots to appear on the foliage of rosebushes. Eventually a yellow halo forms around the black spot, then the entire leaf turns yellow and falls off.	When you prune in spring, throw away all clippings— you'll be throwing away a lot of black spot spores with them. Don't water from overhead. Use a commercial fungicide.
Canker	Canker is a fungus disease that causes canes to die. You will usually notice cankers in the early spring at pruning time; a part of the cane will be healthy but above it will be a black, brown, or purple discoloration. Canker usually enters through a wound.	Canker can't be controlled with chemicals, but you can be careful to prevent wounds. In spring, prune all canes to below any sign of canker.
Japanese beetle	Japanese beetles are shiny copper and green beetles that can devastate the entire garden in a short time. They eat holes in the flowers, and, if hungry enough, will eat the foliage. They're particularly attracted to light-colored flowers.	If you don't have too many Japanese beetles, you can pick them off by hand and destroy them. Traps work, as does the controlling of grubs in the soil with an insecticide.
Leaf rollers	These tiny caterpillars roll themselves up in the rose foliage and eat through it from the inside out. Another telltale sign of these pests is tiny holes in the base of the flower buds.	There are few ways to control them physically, but a commercial insecticide will easily keep them in check.

INSECT/DISEASE	DESCRIPTION AND TROUBLE SIGNS	CONTROL
Midge	A midge is an insect that is actually a tiny maggot which bores into a rose plant, causing the buds and new shoots to suddenly blacken.	When you see signs of midge, prune out the damaged pieces immediately and discard. Some commercial insecticides will put a stop to midge.
Mildew	When a white powder forms on rosebuds and leaves, you have a case of mildew. It is most prevalent when cool nights follow warm days, or where air circulation is poor. Mildew often causes a serious disfiguration of rose foliage.	If you can plant roses where air circulation is good, you'll eliminate the chances of mildew. A commercial fungicide will work if used as a preventive.
Rust	When the powder on your rosebuds and leaves is orange, you have a disease known as rust. Primarily confined to the West Coast, rust is caused by wet and mild weather.	Before you plant a new rosebush, inspect it carefully for signs of rust and don't plant it if you see any. Control with a commercial fungicide.
Spider mites	You won't be able to see the spider mite, but you will be able to see its devastating effects. It's not an insect, but it does the damage of one. Foliage turns a dull red, and you can see webs in advanced stages. Mites weaken roses by sucking juices from foliage.	The one thing spider mites can't stand is water, so keep the plants well watered and hose down the undersides of the leaves. Miticide can be used three days apart.
Thrips	If the garden should be in bloom but it isn't, you may have thrips—microscopic insects that bore into the petals and suck juices from the flower. Buds become distorted and brown and will not open.	Since thrips hide in the buds and flowers, cut buds off and destroy them. Insecticides applied to the buds and the ground will keep thrips away.

CONSIDER YOUR CLIMATE

The climatic conditions in your area are a mixture of different weather patterns: sun, snow, rain, wind, and humidity. A good gardener is aware of all of the variations in temperature and conditions in his or her own garden, from how much rainfall it receives each year to the high and low temperatures of a typical growing season.

The zone map at *right* gives an approximate range of minimum temperatures across the country. Most plants are rated by these zones for conditions where they grow best.

However, zone boundary lines are not absolute. You can obtain the general information for your area from your state agricultural school or your county extension agent.

Be sure to study the microclimates that characterize your own plot of ground. Land on the south side of your house is bound to be warmer than a constantly shaded area exposed to cold, northwest winds. Being aware of the variations in your garden will help you choose the best plant for the prevailing conditions and avoid disappointment.

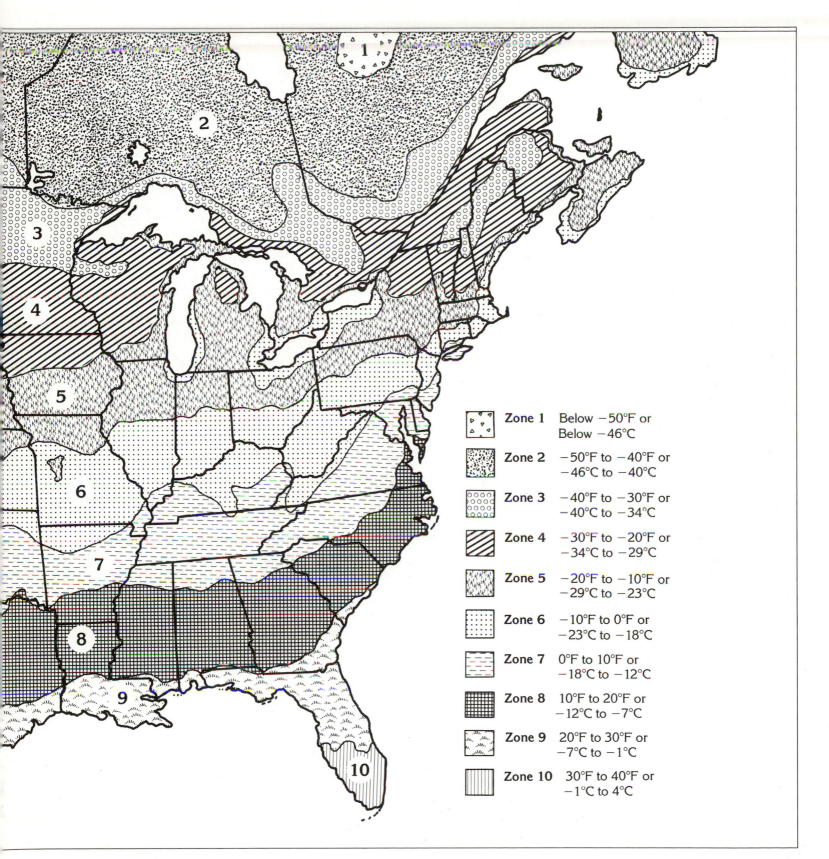

		Zone 1	Below −50°F or Below −46°C
Zone 2	−50°F to −40°F or −46°C to −40°C
Zone 3	−40°F to −30°F or −40°C to −34°C
Zone 4	−30°F to −20°F or −34°C to −29°C
Zone 5	−20°F to −10°F or −29°C to −23°C
Zone 6	−10°F to 0°F or −23°C to −18°C
Zone 7	0°F to 10°F or −18°C to −12°C
Zone 8	10°F to 20°F or −12°C to −7°C
Zone 9	20°F to 30°F or −7°C to −1°C
Zone 10	30°F to 40°F or −1°C to 4°C

INDEX